St. Patrick's Day

Dorothy Rhodes Freeman

Reading Consultant

Michael P. French, Ph.D.,
Bowling Green State University

—Best Holiday Books—

Enslow Publishers, Inc.

40 Industrial Road   PO Box 38
Box 398   Aldershot
Berkeley Heights, NJ 07922   Hants GU12 6BP
USA   UK
http://www.enslow.com

Library of Congress Cataloging-in-Publication Data

Freeman, Dorothy Rhodes.
     St. Patrick's Day / Dorothy Rhodes Freeman.
        p. cm. — (Best holiday books)
     Includes index.
     Summary: Describes the celebration of Saint Patrick's Day which
honors the patron saint of Ireland.
     ISBN 0-89490-383-7
     1. Saint Patrick's Day—Juvenile literature. [1. Saint Patrick's
Day. 2. Patrick, Saint, 373?–463? 3. Saints.] I. Title.
II. Series.
GT4995.P3F74 1992
394.2'6628—dc20   91-43098
                                                 CIP
                                                 AC

Printed in the United States of America

10 9 8

Illustration Credits:
Bonnie Rhodes, pp. 6, 10, 12, 14, 17, 20, 22, 32, 34, 43; Dianne M. MacMillan, p. 40; Irish
Tourist Board, pp. 29, 36; Patricia Woodhull, pp. 25, 26; St. Patrick's Cathedral, New York City,
p. 38; Unicorn Photos, p. 4

Cover Illustration by Charlott Nathan

Contents

Children in a St. Patrick's Day parade.

St. Patrick's Day

St. Patrick's Day is March 17. People all over the world celebrate this day. People march in parades and marching bands play. Some sing Irish songs. Others dance Irish dances. Many people wear green because it is an Irish color. Corned beef and cabbage is a favorite meal on St. Patrick's Day. This day is a joyful time.

Saint Patrick is the patron saint of Ireland. In the Catholic church, a saint is someone who is thought to be very special. A patron saint takes special care of a country or group. The Irish believe that Saint Patrick watches over them.

March 17 is not Patrick's birthday. It is the day of his death. He died around the year A.D. 460. That is over 1,500 years ago. We are not sure of the date.

Patrick wrote down the things that happened to him. This is how we know about his life.

What We Know About Saint Patrick

We know something about Saint Patrick from his own words. When he was an old man, he wrote about his life. He told how he came to Ireland. He described his life there. His writing has been saved for over 1,500 years! In this book there are sentences in quotation marks. They are Patrick's words.

Long ago people learned about the past by listening to stories told by others. Sometimes the stories were true. Sometimes they were made up. When stories are told over and over again they sometimes become legends. Many legends are about Saint Patrick.

It was a long time after Saint Patrick's death before men wrote down these stories. People study Saint Patrick's life. They debate about what is true. They wonder what was made up by the storytellers and writers. As you read about Saint Patrick, you can begin to decide what you think is true!

Patrick Grows Up in Britain

Patrick was born somewhere in Britannia. Britannia is now called Britain. Britain is an island that includes England, Scotland, and Wales. But Patrick was not Irish or British. He was Roman.

A long time ago, much of Britain was ruled by the Roman Empire. Some Romans lived in Britain.

Patrick wrote that he lived by the sea in a large house. We think he was wealthy because he wrote about servants in his house. Britain can be cold and damp. But Patrick's house may have been warm. Romans knew ways to keep a house warm. We know this because there are ruins of Roman houses in Britain.

The countries shown on this map are now called the "British Isles" or "Great Britain." The names of the regions are now England, Scotland, and Wales. In Patrick's time, Ireland was called Hibernia. The large island was called Britannia.

Patrick wrote that he did not study when he was a boy. He did not believe in religion and prayer. He said he did not obey the priests. This was strange because Patrick's grandfather was a priest. His father also worked in the church. Long ago priests could marry. They could have children.

Raiders stole Patrick and some of his family's servants.

Patrick Is Kidnapped

When Patrick was sixteen, his life changed. He was kidnapped!

Across the sea was an island. It was called Hibernia. Now the sea is called the Irish Sea. The island is now called Ireland.

Some fierce men called raiders lived there. They sailed to other lands. They stole people from their homes and sold them as slaves.

The raiders were strong men. They would tie people up and carry them to their ships. The raiders kidnapped Patrick. They also stole some of his family's servants.

The ship sailed to Ireland. There the raiders sold Patrick. An important chief named Miliuc bought him. Patrick was a slave!

Miliuc owned herds of sheep. Patrick had to take care of them. He became a shepherd. He lived outdoors with the sheep. Like Britain, Ireland gets cold and wet. Patrick had no shelter. Perhaps he kept warm among the sheep.

Patrick had no one to talk to. He said he was among "barbarians." Barbarians are wild, cruel people.

Patrick thought God was angry with him. He thought it was because he had not obeyed the

Patrick spent his days caring for Miliuc's sheep.

priests. He began to pray. Sometimes he prayed all night.

Patrick wrote that he lived in the woods and on the mountains. We know shepherds take sheep to the mountains. The sheep graze there in warm weather. They come down in the winter. Patrick said he prayed "through snow, through frost, through rain."

Six years passed. Patrick said prayers day and night. We do not know what he prayed for. Perhaps he asked for strength. Maybe he asked to go home.

One night Patrick heard a voice. It said, "Soon you will go to your own country." The voice spoke again. "See, your ship is ready."

Patrick was miles from the sea. Yet the voice spoke about a ship! Patrick called the voice Victor. Maybe Patrick thought Victor was an angel.

Patrick ran away from Miliuc. He walked 200 miles. He believed God was guiding him. Finally he reached the sea. There was a ship at the shore!

Patrick called to the ship's captain. He begged the captain to take him on board.

People who helped runaway slaves were punished. Perhaps the captain guessed that Patrick was a slave. The captain answered harshly, "It's no use for you to ask."

Patrick could not go back to Miliuc. Slaves who ran away were killed. He started to leave. As he walked, he began to pray.

Perhaps his prayers were heard. Suddenly things changed. Patrick heard one of the ship's crew shouting to him. "Come, hurry. We'll take you. Make friends with us." Patrick went on board. Some believe the ship had a cargo of dogs. They think the dogs were Irish wolfhounds.

Irish wolfhounds were valued as hunters. They can fight a wolf and win. They can outrun big elk. Wolfhounds were shipped from Ireland to Britain. They were sold to wealthy men.

The ship set sail. The captain and crew treated him well. If the ship went to Britain, Patrick might find his way home.

The sailors may have shown Patrick a cargo of Irish wolfhound dogs.
They were probably the largest dogs Patrick had ever seen.

Patrick Saves the Crew From Starving

The ship was blown off its course. It ran aground. The shore was rocky. The men and dogs had to get off the ship.

Patrick and the crew wandered for twenty-eight days. They did not see any people. They did not know where they were. Some think Patrick was in Britain. Others think he landed in a place called Gaul. Gaul is now the countries of France, Belgium, and part of Germany.

The land was deserted. There were no animals to hunt. The food supplies were gone. The men and the dogs were starving.

The captain grabbed Patrick. "You say your God is powerful. Why, then, do you not pray for us. Can't you see we're suffering from hunger?" Patrick told the captain to believe in God. He said God would send food.

Suddenly a herd of wild pigs appeared on the road. The men killed some of them. They ate the meat and got back their strength. The dogs had all they could eat, too. Later the men found wild honey. They stayed at that place two nights.

We are not sure what happened next, but Patrick wrote that he was captured again. He does not say who captured him.

One story says that wild-looking men captured the crew. They sold all but Patrick as slaves. Patrick watched the men. They hunted and fished. They gathered wild foods. Patrick remembered it all.

Another story says Patrick was held captive by the captain. He wanted Patrick with him. He might need Patrick to pray for more food.

Both stories agree that the voice of Victor spoke to Patrick again. It said, "Two months will you be with them."

A gang of men captured Patrick and the ship's crew.

Two months passed. Patrick wrote, "The Lord delivered me out of their hands."

Patrick was free. He had seen what happened when he prayed. It is thought that he then became very religious. Patrick became a priest like his grandfather.

Patrick's vision, Victor, showed Patrick messages from the Irish people. He heard their voices asking him to come back to them once more.

Patrick Returns Home and Leaves Again

Years passed. At last Patrick found his way home. His mother and father welcomed their son. He had been gone so long!

Patrick then had a vision. In it, Victor handed Patrick a letter. Patrick read the first words. They said, "The voice of the Irish." Then Irish voices said, "Come walk among us once more."

His parents begged him not to leave. They said he had suffered so many hardships. They said he should not go away.

But Patrick was willing to return to Ireland. Patrick left home and went to Ireland. He didn't want to leave, but he thought God wanted him to go.

Patrick was made a bishop. Some priests went with him to Ireland.

Patrick's work was to start churches. He was to get Irish people to become Christians. That was sometimes hard to do. Most Irish people believed in spells and magic. They believed in many gods. Many people didn't want to give up their beliefs.

Ireland was ruled by many chiefs. Some call them kings. They were like Miliuc, his former master. Each chief had advisors who were called druids. The druids were wizards who did magic.

The druids said they could see the future. They said that a stranger was coming. They said his teaching would end their way of life. Patrick was a stranger. He did teach another way of living. It is easy to see why the druids were Patrick's enemies.

Patrick's life was often in danger. Druids tried to kill him. Patrick said, "Daily I expect murder, fraud, or captivity." Some chiefs tried

Patrick as imagined in his bishop's robes. He lived a rugged life and seldom dressed like this. He usually wore a long, brown robe and carried a short cane.

Each chief had advisors called druids. A druid could do magic and claimed to tell the future.

to kill Patrick. Once they chained him in irons for fourteen days.

Patrick faced the druids. He got many chiefs to become Christians. He even made priests of some druids. After this, many people became Christians. Patrick said he baptized thousands of Irish people.

Patrick the Saint

Saint Patrick is known as the patron saint of Ireland. The Irish believe that Saint Patrick watches over them. They believe that he will decide if they can get into heaven.

Saint Patrick is often called the best-loved saint. People go to church to honor him. Even people who do not believe in religion celebrate his day. Why is he so loved and so popular?

The answer is that he was a very loving person. He was kidnapped and sold. He was made a slave. But he didn't become mean or bitter. He didn't hate the raiders or Miliuc. When he was an old man, he wrote, "I have mercy on the people who once took me captive."

A view of the Irish countryside. The Irish believe Saint Patrick takes special care of Ireland.

Patrick could have had an easy life in Britain. Instead, he went back to Ireland. He wrote, "I came to the people of Ireland to give up my free birth for the benefit of others." We know he cared about people and for the Irish.

Legends About Saint Patrick

Storytellers told many other stories about Patrick. One legend tells about Patrick and the snakes of Ireland.

The legend says Patrick charmed all the snakes in Ireland. When he walked to the sea, all the snakes followed him. When they came to the sea, all the snakes swam away from Ireland. Ireland was rid of snakes forever.

On St. Patrick's Day people talk about the "wearing of the green." They may wear green clothing, or pin on a green ribbon. They wear green because of the legend of the shamrock.

Legend has it that Patrick was preaching about the Father, the Son, and the Holy Spirit.

Patrick was telling them that all three made up one God. Some people questioned him. Why did Patrick say there was one God and worship three?

The legend says Patrick bent down. He picked a green shamrock. It was the leaf of a clover plant. He held it out, showing its leaf. The leaf had three round parts. The three parts were all part of one leaf. He compared the three parts that made one leaf of the shamrock to the three parts that made one God. The shamrock leaf became a symbol of Saint Patrick.

A legend says that Saint Patrick drove the snakes from Ireland.

The Irish believe shamrocks bring good luck. They think shamrocks protect a person from evil spirits. A girl might put a shamrock in her lover's shoe. This was to make sure he would return to her. Some Irish people who came to America carried shamrocks for good luck.

Another legend is about fairies and leprechauns (LEP-reh-kons). Irish people used to believe in magic spirits. Over time, the spirits became less important to the Irish. The spirits got smaller and become the "wee ones" or little people. These are the fairies.

It is said that fairies love to dance. They wear out a lot of shoes. Some of the wee ones are men dressed in green. These are the leprechauns. They carry a shoemaker's hammer and mend the fairies' shoes.

Leprechauns are said to be grouchy and mean. They prefer to live alone. Leprechauns work at night while the fairies sleep. The fairies pay the leprechauns with gold.

Leprechauns collect pots of gold which they hide. Legend says that if you catch one, he will lead you to his pot of gold. To find him, you can listen for the tap of his tiny hammer. But if you catch a leprechaun, don't take your eyes off him. Otherwise, he will be gone in a second.

Patrick never saw a leprechaun, but the gentle saint might have smiled at the stories. Leprechauns do not look grouchy in pictures now. They usually look jolly. They may be dancing an Irish dance called a jig.

The leprechaun repairs the fairies' shoes. He works at night while the fairies sleep. Fairies dance and wear out a lot of shoes.

St. Patrick's Day Celebrations

St. Patrick's Day started many years after Patrick died. Today, there are many ways people like to celebrate.

In Ireland, St. Patrick's Day is a holy day. Most people go to church. Then they spend time with family and friends. Sometimes they meet in a pub. This is like a restaurant and bar. They drink to Saint Patrick.

The first St. Patrick's Day celebration in the United States was in 1737. It took place in Boston. Many of the people there were from Ireland.

One way people like to celebrate St. Patrick's Day is to march in or watch parades. Thousands of people in towns and cities all over the world have parades on St. Patrick's Day. The parades began in New York City in the 1700s. The New York parade is still the longest.

There is also a big parade in Sydney, Australia. In Sydney, March 17 is nicknamed "Saint Paddy's Day." There are other St. Patrick's Day parades in cities in Canada,

There are parades on St. Patrick's Day all over the world. This man is leading a parade in Dublin, Ireland.

Africa, and South America. Even some cities in Ireland have parades now. Sometimes marching bands from the United States go to Ireland to play in parades.

Lots of people sing Irish songs on St. Patrick's Day. One of the most popular songs is called "When Irish Eyes Are Smilin'." Another is called "The Wearin' of the Green."

Some cities celebrate St. Patrick's Day by doing unusual things. In Chicago, some people color the water of the Chicago River green in honor of Saint Patrick. People in San Antonio, Texas, do the same thing with the San Antonio River.

In New York City, the Empire State Building lights the night sky with green lights for the holiday.

The town of Shamrock, Florida was named after the shamrocks found in Ireland. Each St. Patrick's Day, many people send letters to be mailed from the post office there. That way, the postmark will say "Shamrock."

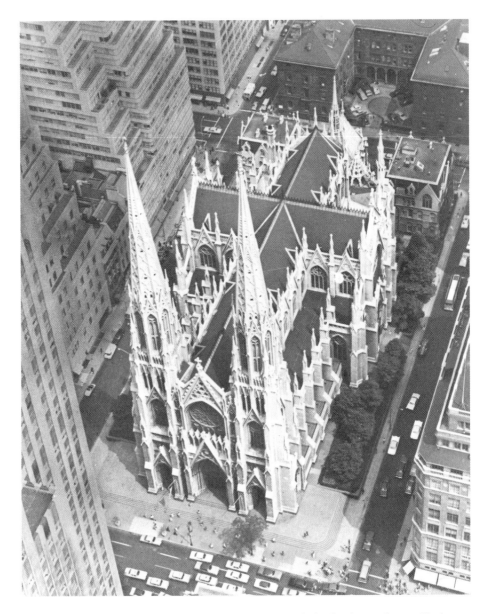

St. Patrick's Cathedral in New York City, as it looks from above. Each year, a parade honoring Saint Patrick passes in front of this cathedral.

Even some businesses join the celebration. Sometimes car washes give a free wash to green cars on St. Patrick's Day. Or a dry cleaner may clean green garments for free.

People honor Saint Patrick by naming cathedrals for him. A cathedral is a large church. Famous ones are in Dublin, Ireland and in New York City.

These children are in a school in Ocean View School District in Orange County, California. They made leprechauns to celebrate St. Patrick's Day.

St. Patrick's Day
in a School

Many schools celebrate St. Patrick's Day. Children wear something green. Some wear all green clothing. Others pin on something green. It might be a ribbon or a clover.

In one school, students found small green footprints at the classroom door. The footprints led into a cupboard. Maybe a leprechaun could be found inside! The children hunted for the leprechaun who had left the tracks.

In the cupboard, they found only a tiny shoe and cookies shaped like shamrocks. They ate the cookies. Then they made leprechauns from green paper. Their teacher told them about Saint Patrick. Then she taught them an Irish dance and an Irish song.

Symbols of Saint Patrick and Ireland

A symbol is something that stands for another thing. The shamrock is a symbol for Saint Patrick.

Flags are symbols for countries. The Irish flag has three stripes. The stripes run across the flag. The top stripe is orange. It is for the people of northern Ireland. The bottom stripe is green. It is for the people of southern Ireland.

For many years the Irish of the south and north have been fighting. The middle stripe of the flag is white. It stands for hope. The hope is that the two parts of Ireland will stop fighting. It is a hope for peace.

The Irish harp is also a symbol of Ireland.

There is another Irish flag. It is not the official flag. It has a green background. In the center is a golden Irish harp.

The Irish harp is another symbol of Ireland. A harp is a musical instrument with strings to pluck. Long ago, the harp was played while storytellers told tales. The harps were small. They had a sweet tone. Some harps were decorated with shamrocks.

If Patrick were alive now, he might enjoy a parade. He might wear his bishop's robe. He might hold a shamrock. Perhaps he would eat corned beef and cabbage. He might join in singing Irish songs while a harpist played.

Glossary

A.D.—An abbreviation for *Anno Domini*, Latin for "in the year of the Lord." It refers to years after the birth of Jesus.

advisors—Persons who help others make decisions.

bishop—A rank above a priest in some Christian churches.

Britannia—The ancient name for the island that now includes England, Scotland, and Wales.

cathedral—A very large church; it may be the church headed by a bishop.

druids—Men who advised the Irish chiefs.

empire—All the lands ruled by an emperor.

Gaul—The European nation that is now the countries of France, Belgium, and part of Germany.

Hibernia—The ancient name for Ireland.

Ireland—An island country west of Britain.

irons—Iron bracelets or leg cuffs.

legend—A story that was told over and over before it was written down. A legend may or may not be true.

leprechaun—A legendary little man who mends fairies' shoes.

patron saint—A saint who takes special care of a country or group.

priest—A minister in some Christian churches.

raiders—Fierce men who stole people and sold them as slaves.

Romans—People from the old empire of Rome.

saint—A holy person who has died, and is honored by the church for his or her very good life. The abbreviation for saint is "St."

St. Patrick's Day—March 17, the day that is celebrated in Saint Patrick's honor.

shamrock—A type of clover plant with three leaves.

symbol—A thing that stands for a person, place, or idea.

wolfhound—A type of dog that is very large and shaggy.

Index